A CELEBRATION OF WESTERN CANADIAN NATURE

WILDERNESS ODYSSEY

A CELEBRATION OF WESTERN CANADIAN NATURE

WILDERNESS ODYSSEY

From the vast, fertile Prairies to the immense, blue Pacific.
From the American border to the white, severe Arctic.
Plains, mountains, great rivers and lakes,
abundant wildlife, unmatched beauty of landscape.
Western Canada
WILDERNESS ODYSSEY

G B PUBLISHING

Photographic studies of George Brybycin:

THE HIGH ROCKIES
COLOURFUL CALGARY I
OUR FRAGILE WILDERNESS
THE ROCKY MOUNTAINS
BANFF NATIONAL PARK
JASPER NATIONAL PARK
COLOURFUL CALGARY II
WILDLIFE IN THE ROCKIES
ROCKY MOUNTAIN SYMPHONY
ENCHANTED WILDERNESS
WILDERNESS ODYSSEY

Editor: Dorothy Dickson
Layout and design: George Brybycin

First Edition 1986

ISBN 0-919029-11-6   Hard Cover

G B PUBLISHING
Box 6292 Station D
Calgary, Alberta
Canada T2P 2C9

Front cover: Moraine Lake, Banff National Park

A CELEBRATION OF WESTERN CANADIAN NATURE

WILDERNESS ODYSSEY

text:

DOROTHY DICKSON

photographs:

GEORGE BRYBYCIN

Twenty years ago, I looked on with pleasure as my five-year old daughter discovered the fascination of watching ants. She was lying in a forest clearing some distance from where I was cooking our camp supper and was so intrigued that she did not even look up at the red squirrel scolding her from the branch above.

* * *

As adults, our enchantment with the wilderness is often dependent on magnificent scenery or seeing the larger mammals and birds. Tiers of snowy mountains resplendent in the sun, brilliantly hued lakes, herds of elk or caribou, thousands of snow geese swirling against a blue sky — the great sights of the wild lands give us a thrill and lift our spirits above the drab concerns of daily life. But perhaps we need, at least sometimes, to join the children on the forest floor and be reminded that without the work of little things, the life of the vast vistas we enjoy could not survive.

Do not worry that delving into the private lives of the tiny plants and animals around us will make the wilderness seem too ordered and scientific and take away the magic. Looking at nature through even a simple magnifying glass opens up a whole new world of enchantment. Lie down and examine the ground round you or look closely at that nearby chunk of rock. The chances are good that you will find a lichen.

These pioneers of the plant world are usually the first to colonize a newly formed or altered landscape. They are actually composed of two plants, a fungus and an alga growing together for their mutual benefit, a situation known as symbiosis. The lichens gradually — so very gradually — break down the rock and help to form soil. It may take one of the crustose lichens that form grey, orange, green or yellow patches on rocks hundreds of years to grow to one foot across. So treat with respect this ancient denizen of the wilderness that was already growing long before white man explored the Rockies.

You will also find lichens that have leaf-like structures. These foliose lichens are often seen growing on trees or doing their job of slowly breaking up fallen logs. The fruticose or shrubby lichens are most attractive with their bushy gold, green or grey 'beards' hanging from the trees or tiny 'pixie cups' growing on logs or soil among the debris of the forest floor.

Lichens have uses in nature other than breaking down soil particles so that higher plants can take root. They provide food and shelter for insects. Mammals large and small feed on them and man has used them for dyes, in the manufacture of antibiotics and, more recently, as an 'early-warning system' for some forms of air pollution to which lichens are particularly sensitive.

Like most people, I enjoy flowers and accepted, with pleasure but not much thought, the wide range of shapes and colours the more obvious ones exhibit. Then, one day I was walking through some boring scrub on a dull morning in early spring. I tripped over a twisted root and my head came level with the bare branches of a

buffalo-berry bush. Bare? I knelt in the mud and looked in amazement at the branches covered with minute flowers. How could I have missed seeing them before? There
in the 'boring' scrub was all the charm and beauty one could ask for just waiting to
be found.

The branches of the bush looked as though they had been brushed with gold
dust. The leaves were closed in pairs like tiny hands held in prayer as they waited
for sun and moisture to let them grow and spread. The neat little flowers had yellow-
green sepals forming a four-pointed star round the yellow-tipped stamens. On the
next bush, however, the flowers had no stamens, only the single spike of the female
pistil waiting to be fertilized.

The discovery of the buffalo-berry flowers sent us on a quest for other tiny
beauties. There is obviously an art in finding them. You must move slowly and be
very observant for they are to be found from the tallest trees to flat on the earth. We
discovered that the elm and maple trees in our own garden carry most attractive flower
clusters that we had merely glanced at before. We found Fairy Candelabra spreading
its slim stems and pale 2 mm. blossoms over many places we had thought were bare.
One tiny flower we sought for a long time was the Mitella, also known as Bishop's
Cap or Mitrewort because of the shape of its unopened seed capsule. Once the
capsule opens, however, it looks more like a minute bird's nest with the tiny black
seeds for eggs. The day we found it, we were as triumphant as if we had found gold.
As so often happens, once we had found them, we kept on doing so, wondering how
we could have been so unobservant before. The flower is very dainty with its petals
split into filaments which form a gossamer halo and look rather like a green spider's
web.

Spiders' webs themselves are one of the most delightful things added to the
scene by the tiny creatures we usually overlook unless they annoy us. Even spiders'
threads can be an annoyance at times, as anyone who has been the first to walk
along a wilderness trail in the morning well knows. The slightly sticky, invisible
strands stretched across the path cling to your face, clothes and binoculars. But then
I remember the early morning when we were driving down a back road in northern
Alberta. It was late August and the dying plants on the wide verge were brown and
stiff. Then rays of the rising sun suddenly illuminated the scene from behind and
the roadsides became a fairyland of shining gossamer threads in many designs alive
with the flashing rainbow lights of sunlit dew. The dark forest edge made a perfect
background to an enchanted scene which only lasted a few moments but became
a memory to last a lifetime.

There are thought to be more than 120,000 species of spiders in the world
and if they were not there to keep the insects in check, none of the larger animals
— such as ourselves — could exist. Insects make up more than half all animals on
earth and most are capable of reproducing so rapidly that we would soon be over-run
and the world stripped of vegetation if they were left to breed without constraint.
The numbers involved are so colossal as to be almost beyond comprehension. There

may be hundreds of species and many thousands of individuals on an acre of land. That they have to utilize the same crops as grazing animals is often overlooked. How many caterpillars equal one elk, I wonder, in the competition for food? Without the insects, would there be any food for the elk?

We often think of insects only as pests. They damage our growing crops, contaminate food, spread disease and hurt or annoy us with their bites and stings. However, many species are beneficial. Crops which may be harmed by some insects may rely on others for pollination, without which they could not produce their fruits to feed us. Insects give us honey and silk. They are essential food for many birds, mammals and fish. They are very efficient scavengers, clearing up dead or decaying plant and animal matter and aiding in the recycling of nutrients. Some of them help to keep others under control by eating or parasitizing them. Helpful or harmful, beautiful or bizarre, the variety is so great that learning about insects is an adventure in itself.

Butterflies and moths are the glamorous stars of the insect world. The big ones are often lovely but I think the little ones give me most pleasure, especially the dainty blues which dance over the alpine meadows with their less showy, but still elegant, mates. It pleases me that some past entomologist whimsically named these sprites the 'gossamer wings' instead of using some more mundane terminology for them.

Compared to the fluttering of the butterflies, the direct flight of the dragon and damsel flies seems harsh and strong. The light catches their shining colours as they dart in all directions to grab mosquitoes and flies in mid-air. I also enjoy the aptly-named lacewings. Their delicate-looking wings are surely one of the purest greens in nature. It is nice to know, too, that they are helping the ladybugs to keep my garden aphids in check.

Even the humble aphids present a fascinating story. Their eggs hatch in the spring but produce only wingless females. These, having no mates, give birth to generations of live clones all summer but as the weather gets colder and the days get shorter, the last generation produced can fly and has both sexes. These mate and lay the eggs from which the cycle starts again the next spring. Some of the eggs are collected by ants which incubate them in their nest all winter and then take the young aphids back to the correct food plant in the spring. As the aphids eat, grow and reproduce, the ants 'milk' them for their secretions.

Nature is often amazingly complex as species have evolved to make use of or defend themselves against other species. The more we learn, the more we discover how interwoven are the lives of different plants and animals, all combining in one long odyssey from when life on earth began and reaching, entwined, into the future. Thus, while we might, indeed, be over-run with insects if they were not preyed upon by so many other forms of life, we nevertheless could not survive without them.

Flight is probably the ability we most envy in other creatures, particularly the lazy soaring of the bigger birds. Who has not longed to glide with the eagle as it drifts from peak to peak, covering in effortless seconds a distance that would take us laborious days. Have you ever seen a spiral staircase of white pelicans climbing into a blue prairie sky? Or the arrowhead streamers of geese and swans cutting their way so purposefully to the spacious north or the warm south? It is easy to forget the hazards they face and long to fling yourself up in the air to join them. I always experience a great sense of loss and loneliness as the excited clamour of migrating skeins fades into the distance, leaving me earthbound and dissatisfied.

The gay colours of many birds are a renewed joy each spring and the more subtle shadings and markings of others, even the common house sparrow, are beautiful. There are, however, two rather sombre-looking birds that please and intrigue me. In contrast to their funereal garb, ravens seem to have so much fun! They attack life with raucous exuberance, soaring, diving, tumbling around the skies and missing nothing that goes on below them. They make an astonishing variety of sounds, from the familiar, arrogantly harsh 'kronk' and barklike croaks to such gently muted crooning that it is hard to believe all could come from the same birds. Contrasts and its apparent joie de vivre make the drab dipper endearing too — a land bird that can walk and fly under water, a little bird of the mountains that does not migrate to warmer climes and, most of all, the bird that can make an unknowing winter traveller gasp in astonishment at its sudden burst of loud, bubbling song. I'm sure there is a serious purpose for the song, such as establishing a winter feeding territory, but who cares what the reason when that joyous carol rings out to warm your heart on a dull, cold day. I feel a real sense of gratitude to the jaunty little dippers and to the other birds which cheer us by braving the winter weather in our company.

Birds are not our only singers. The merry song of the peepers is one of the first signs springs has at last come to the prairies. Have you ever noticed that each frog chorus seems to have a conductor who can make hundreds of voices stop and re-start in perfect synchrony? As so often happens in nature, the facts in this case are as intriguing as the fantasy. It is now believed that frogs are acutely sensitive to vibrations transmitted through the ground. So they don't have to hear or see you coming to make them fall silent, they can all feel your approach through their feet!

Sound is surely one of the most enchanting aspects of nature: the songs and sounds of birds, insects, amphibians, the calls of the mammals — male to female, parents to young; cheerful greetings, boastful challenges, hungry cries, cries of fear or pain, of warning and of triumph. Wind whispers and roars. Water chuckles in a mountain stream, thunders over the cliff edge or crashes in great waves on the shore only to chuckle again as it is sucked back over the water-bright pebbles to rejoin the sea. Ice tinkles on the trees in the winter breeze but the lake creaks and groans at the coming of spring. Rain on canvas. Rain on leaves. Hail drumming on the sun-baked earth, pounding plants to pulp, harsh, cold and unforgiving in the warmth of summer. Lightning crackles as it slits the sky to herald the thunder's roll. Frightening, exciting, awesome. So peaceful when it is over and a deep hush descends.

Never push the silence of nature away. Become a part of it. Then discover that the land is never quite silent. There is always the flutter of a wing, the rustle in the grass giving away the ever-present life we seldom notice. The tiny sounds, like the tiny sights, are delightful, even if not as thrilling as the howl of the wolf or the plaint of the loon.

Sound will often give away the presence of creatures we cannot see. I remember tip-toeing past a reed bed in a canoe as the dawn mists were rising from the lake and eavesdropping on the family chatter of hundreds of ducks and grebes. The soft conversational tones were very different from the raucous cries heard on the open water later in the day. Sometimes it is hard to find the animal you can hear because it is so well camouflaged. One evening we searched and searched for whatever was making an odd creaking sound near our tent. Eventually we located a large beetle, almost invisible against the rough bark of a pine tree. I was so glad we had found it before it was dark or I would have been listening and wondering all night as it hopefully rasped out its mating call.

The small sounds of the night can be so frustrating and so deceptive as our overstretched ears and imaginations put bear-sized bodies behind the scratching of mice. Those alarming rustlings of the dawn become friendly and our fears laughable as the sunrise reveals the silhouette of the chipmunk scrambling and sliding on the slopes of the tent.

Darkness adds a slight feeling of apprehension and vulnerability that makes night noises exciting. Not that the wolves or loons need to be made any more thrilling when their calls fill the night! I once heard the mating calls of a female cougar, calls which started with low moans and rose to a frenzied scream that ended abruptly and left the night holding its breath as everything waited in a tremulous hush for the cry to come again. The lull after such an explosion of sound seems much deeper than the usual quietness of the night but it is a silence quivering with anxiety and lacks the feeling of peace that so often comes as darkness descends over the wilderness.

On a calm night, I find the stillness almost overwhelming, making the universe around me seem limitless and myself so very small. Then I look up at those far away stars and my own insignificance is accentuated even more. At the same time, the stars give me a feeling of being part of a great continuity. Those are the stars all the living things that have ever existed in our hemisphere have looked up to. The stars seem to connect me to the past more than anything on earth — to the beginnings of life, to the dinosaurs, to the first men and, above all, to the men who have been able to articulate their wonder. Those are the stars that guided Hannibal, that inspired Chaucer, intrigued Galileo, that lit Shakespeare home after a night at the theatre. And measured by the life of the wilderness around me, they all saw those stars shine but an instant ago. If I could but wish upon a star with the faith of a child, it would be to ensure that the wilderness, with all its wonder, will still be there to enchant my descendants hundreds of years in the future.

The coming of each dawn is celebrated slowly in the cold of winter. Except for the impatient ravens, the few birds bestir themselves gradually as the sun's warmth makes movement easier or hunger drives them to seek food whatever the weather. Everything seems to stretch slowly — do I have to get up? But in spring the birds and small mammals can hardly wait to start a new day and I find the mood is catching. Early morning is certainly the best time to be about and see the activity of the wilderness. An area that had seemed devoid of wildlife one mid-day was all a-bustle as we hiked through the next morning. Most intriguing were the varied thrushes. There seemed to be dozens of them, each with its own favourite note. I remember the first time we heard a varied thrush. We didn't know where to look or what to look for, so weird the sound seemed. We finally sat on a log beside a moss-rimmed pool and searched everywhere through our binoculars. We passed over the 'robin' perched on top of a spruce tree. It was some time before we were really convinced that this bird was making the eldritch cries. Another of those wilderness mysteries that it is almost a shame to solve! But another memory to hold dear.

It is a happy coincidence that some of the early birds to arrive in the spring are among the most colourful and gay. Bluebirds arrive with the summer sky on their backs and warblers show off the patches of sunshine on their heads, wings and rumps. They are a fitting introduction to the renewed colours of spring and summer and are soon followed by the vivid orange-gold and black orioles and the looping, twittering goldfinches dressed in a softer lemon-gold to contrast with their black wings and tails. Hummingbirds flash their jewel-bright feathers as they hover to sip sweet nectar and then back away to dart to the next bloom.

The tree buds that we have gratefully watched all winter with their reassurance that spring will come, sprinkle, then cloak the trees with such fresh greens that your heart cannot help but respond with delight. The soft purples of the prairie crocuses peer out from their silky shawls on a sun-warmed slope and the succession of plants is set in motion again.

Spring creeps up the mountainsides and north on to the tundra. It is there that the colourful parade of species is most noticeable — sheets of creamy-white followed in a few days by yellows, then blues with brilliant patches of pink interspersed. When you have only a few days to live your efforts to attract passing pollinators must be spectacular or you will have no descendants. This is why the blossoms in the alpine and arctic regions so often appear almost ridiculously large for the plants that produce them. Others, such as moss campion, rely on massed blooms to shout their wares to the merchant insects. While stalks and leaves are often small and sometimes hairy to keep them warm and moist, the roots of many alpine plants are, like the flowers, disproportionately large, thrusting deeply or spreading widely into the rocky ground to reach for moisture or to hold the plant safely anchored in the blustering winds. The way plants have adapted to survive in harsh environments is a most fascinating subject to study.

The tundra that is uniformly snow white and, except for the wind, quiet for so much of the year, certainly makes up for it in the brief spring and summer. It would be hard to imagine any habitat more replete with the colour and sounds of life. With the massed flowers as frames, every lake and slough attracts its quota of geese, ducks and waders coming home to perform their elaborate and often noisy courtship rituals. As breeding territories are claimed, the air is full of voices, from the challenging bugle of the cranes to the melodic trills of the longspurs and pipits, from the cackling laughter of the oldsquaws to the sweet tooraloo of the golden plovers. Peace descends as nest sites are soon established. Even with the help of long hours of daylight, there is no time to waste if the birds are to raise their young and fuel up in time for the long flight south again in the fall. As they leave, the tundra flares red and gold with the turning leaves of bearberry and the miniature birch and willow trees. Further south, where the forests begin, the flare is caught by the larch trees, like candle flames among the dark firs as autumn spreads its fire southwards leaving the cold ashes of winter in its wake.

While many birds and some insects and bats are able to fly south to escape our rigorous winter weather, the animals that stay have developed a variety of strategies to enable them to cope with the cold temperatures and extensive snow cover. Some, such as mice, make use of the fact that temperatures are higher under the white blanket, so they travel and feed in tunnels under the snow. The ground squirrels and marmots retire to prepared chambers deep underground where they can hibernate, happily oblivious to the frigid conditions above. Beavers build up their dams to make sure their ponds are deep enough not to freeze to the bottom where they have a larder full of branches from the trees they have felled. The great bears, with a thick layer of fat stored under their shaggy coats, slow down their metabolism and dream away the cold days in their dens but the feisty little pikas, those round-eared mini-rabbits of the high mountains, still scuttle among the rocks under the snow. They spend the fall cutting plants to dry in the sun and collecting them into 'haystacks' for winter provisions. When there is a lot of snow, some animals such as deer and rabbits change their diets, eating twigs, buds and bark. As the snow deepens and packs hard, they are able to reach higher into the trees. Their predators follow them to the shelter of the forests. Bighorn sheep may still feed above the treeline as they pass down from generation to generation the knowledge of where to find slopes that are swept bare of snow by the wind. Most astonishing of all are those dwellers on top of the world, the mountain goats. They not only scorn dormancy, most of them do not even come far down from their lofty summer homes. Life indeed seems to be tough for the shaggy white mountaineers and in a bad winter their losses can be heavy. Yet they have managed to evolve to fit a 'niche' that no other animal can tolerate and they rarely have to contend with predators in the world's attic.

Like the seasons, weather can make the look and mood of an area change completely. A sparkling white fairyland can be turned into a menacing expanse of ice and snow merely by a cloud passing across the sun. But stormy or even wet and misty weather can somehow suit and enhance wild scenery. The sweep of a storm across the mountains conveys a thrill of its own, while mist swirling down the cliffs or creeping fitfully among the trees brings mystery and a straining of the senses which can be exhilarating. Nowhere is the effect of weather more noticeable than on the coast where the rocking-cradle of the sea one day can become the exciting terror of crashing mountains of water the next.

As any photographer can attest, clouds make an ordinary scene spectacular: streamers and wisps of cloud catching the gold and red of a prairie sunrise or sunset and doubling the effect in the looking-glass lakes: the cottonwool fluff of peaceful clouds floating on the heat of a summer day; the dark skyscraper-building menace of a storm cloud looming over the high mountains.

It was on a stormy day on a high plateau that I experienced one of those moments of magic that make the wilderness seem enchanted indeed. Steely masses of cloud swelled above the darkened mountains which rose on either side of a narrow valley entrance. The leaden, white-flecked waters of a mountain stream tumbled over the boulder-strewn opening. Looking down from my vantage point, I could see through the gap to where the valley widened a little and the stream became more sedate. Beyond, all was obscured by a curtain of rain. Suddenly the sun found a crack in the dark canopy and a perfect rainbow arched across the narrow opening while a finger of sunlight pointed out a patch of blue lupins on the valley floor. I kept very still and tried to etch the scene on to my memory, knowing that never again would I or anyone else see it looking so wondrously radiant.

The most enchanted times of all are when the sun comes out after the rain or snow has stopped and a landscape that seemed inhospitable, even threatening, becomes shining and friendly once more. We would not appreciate these times nearly as much if the sun always shone. Contrast is one of the essential ingredients of the wilderness.

It is after rain that the scents and smells of the countryside most often attract our attention. The sense of smell is neglected by most of us and I sometimes wonder what it must be like to be aware of one's surroundings mostly through your nose as so many animals are. It is hard to imagine being able to detect something in the next valley by its smell. Certainly it seems a much more efficient way of surviving in the wild than by eyesight, unless you view the world mostly from above like the keen-eyed goats and eagles. I think it would be nice to have at least one sense that was superbly efficient instead of just five mediocre ones. Our ancestors must have been able to use their senses well enough to survive in the wild, so perhaps with practice we can at least improve and sharpen our often bumbling awareness of what is going on around us. I always have the feeling I am missing so much!

It rather surprises me that smells can be stored so accurately in our memories. Who, having once lived by the sea, does not dream about and miss that salty tang? However large and however high its waves are whipped, a lake is just not good enough because it does not have the right smell. The vastness of the seas and, even with knowledge gained from films of underwater life, the many mysteries of its depths, make the ocean wilderness fascinating to man. The contrast of the beauty and colour of many water plants and fish with the grotesque look and actions of such creatures as lobsters adds to the ocean's spell, making it seem almost like a storybook land of fantasy. The grace of movement in water, be it of waving fronds of seaweed, the sinuous fluency of seals or the lazy strength of whales, is a joy to see.

For many, whales are the most admired of all mammals. Their ability to live where others cannot, their intelligence, gentleness and friendly inquisitiveness all add to their charm. Their size alone inspires our awe. I was once in a boat surrounded by humpback whales, any one of which could have capsized us with an easy heave of its 15 metre body. One swam alongside, looking up at us and slapping the water with its long, scalloped flipper. Everyone was thrilled but I had the uneasy feeling that he was trying to tell us that he had had enough of his resonant underworld being disturbed by engine-throbbing boats and would we please go away. I cannot but wonder if we are putting too much pressure on the gentle giants even when we mean them no harm. Our noises must constantly abuse their acute hearing and interfere with their sophisticated system of vocal communication and use of echo-location. One day their annoyance may erupt into action and they, like the grizzlies, will be labelled 'dangerous'. It will be our own fault but they will be the ones to suffer.

Whether at sea or on land, it is usually the big animals that people are most thrilled to see, perhaps because we are lazy and they are so visible but mainly, I think, because we feel there is a slight element of danger involved in meeting them. When I stalk an animal I am never sure whether it is more satisfying to get close and watch and then get away again without the animal ever realizing I was there or to make my presence known and gradually be accepted without causing alarm. Occasionally I have found myself the one being watched. I particularly remember the day I sat drowsily on some sun-warmed boulders humming quietly to myself. I roused to discover I had an audience of young marmots which gradually edged closer until, their curiosity assuaged or their courage failing, they suddenly scuttered away.

I have had other strange encounters with marmots. One insisted on climbing my legs to lick my jeans, presumably for saltiness left by sweat or a food spatter. When I pushed it down because its claws were scratching me, it was in no way deterred so I sat down and let it lick away in comfort! Another one tried to pull my husband's walking stick out of his hand. Like bears, marmots seem to be quite strict with their babies and I saw one youngster soundly cuffed by father because it did not come when called. Marmots are one of my favourite animals and as I clamber upwards their 'stranger approaching' whistles beckon me on and renew my flagging energy. The areas where marmots live are some of the most attractive in the mountains, flower spangled meadows strewn with boulders fallen from the cliffs above — cliffs where the goats so nimbly climb and the eagles have their nests.

Bighorn sheep also frequent these lovely meadows and one of the most stirring sights is a line of rams wending its way up the mountainside. How enormously strong their neck muscles must be to support those great coiling horns. The re- sounding 'thwack' when two rams meet head on in the rutting season makes me wince. No wonder they need reinforced skulls. The antlers of the deer family are also a great weight to carry. They have time to adjust to the growing load as the antlers develop each year but it must feel an odd change in balance when the antlers are suddenly discarded. You would think that carrying a wide spread as moose and elk have to do would severely hinder their movement among trees, but it does not seem to slow them down much. Moose in particular are amazingly adept at melting quietly into the forest. How often, I wonder, do they and the other animals silently watch us go by without seeing them?

Unfortunately there are no longer many caribou left in the mountains. The autumn males are a magnificent sight. Larger than their arctic cousins, they have silvery manes against a dark coat and long, elegantly curving antlers. Herds are still found in the northern mountains and it was there that I saw them being hunted by wolves.

These big dogs always attract me. They have a pride and self-assurance about them I admire. The power and grace of a wolf running at full stretch are unmatched by any tame dog. I shall never forget the first one I saw. Two swans were lazily floating in a small, glass-smooth arctic lake. A few musk oxen grazed on a distant hillside and a thrush's sweet song rang out in the still air. It was just before midnight and as the sun touched the horizon, golden streaks of sunlight alternated with deep shadow, emphasizing the rolling nature of the land. A wolf moved up the ridge at a long-limbed, swinging trot. As he paused on the sun-bright crest, his white coat flared gold for a moment before he moved on down the other side to drink at the lake and continue on his way.

Another scene equally idyllic and sharply imprinted on my memory comes to mind. We were camped on the side of a pretty little valley which rose up to a boulder strewn marmot meadow. After supper I strolled away from the tents and sat in the evening sun. My eyes wandered lazily from the fluffy clouds down over a rocky crest to the strip of trees on the opposite slope. Below, the backs of our riding and pack horses came into view as they munched peacefully in a meadow by the stream and I wondered idly why one was grazing a little apart from the others. But wait! We don't have a horse that colour. My eyes shot back. The eleventh 'horse' was a grizzly. I was somewhat startled but obviously neither horses nor bear felt in any way threatened and all ate contentedly until dusk when the king of the valley moved up into the trees. He came back two days later and stood a few hundred metres away watching us pack up camp. The humans found it slightly unnerving but the horses were quite uncon- cerned. They obviously must be used to bears around — bears that we have no idea are there.

However magnificent the scenery, however beautiful the flowers, the wilderness would certainly lose its enchantment for most of us if the animals were not there, whether we see them or not.

The greatest attraction the wilderness holds is the constant expectation that the unexpected is about to happen. We are drawn to see over the next ridge, round the next bend in the trail, always hoping that the next step in our wilderness odyssey will reveal a special beauty or bring another intriguing encounter. Even if we know the scenery ahead, it will never have looked quite the same before and there is always the suspense of not knowing if there will be animals there. Will I at last see the wolverine that has always eluded me? Will there be sheep in the next meadow? Goats or an eagle on the cliff? Will a moose appear across the lake? Is there a bear round that corner? I am never quite sure whether I hope there is or not. I am, however, quite sure that if I am not prepared to accept the fact that there might be, I should not be there. I know, too, that if I knew there was not, much of my enchantment with the wilderness would be lost.

*   *   *

Looking from my kitchen window one day last summer, I saw my three-year-old granddaughter crouched on the grass staring intently at something in the flower bed. Quietly I went to kneel beside her but could see nothing special until she pointed to the little bright yellow spider crouched in its camouflage on a bright yellow pansy. With outstretched legs it waited for an unwary fly. Happily I went back to the house but I don't think she even noticed me leave. A new generation was starting a personal odyssey into the enchanted world of nature.

I must remember to buy her a magnifying glass for Christmas.

DOROTHY DICKSON

P · L · A · T · E · S

Bald eagle (Haliaeetus leucocephalus)

Calypso orchid (Calypso bulbosa)

"Annual festival of colours". Larch Valley west of Moraine Lake. Banff National Park, Alberta.

Mirror-like pond near Dawson City surrounded by Yukon's golden autumn scenery.

*Glacier lily (Erythronium grandiflorum). Found in the mountains of southern Alberta and British Columbia.
This photograph was taken near Revelstoke. The Monashee Mountains provide the background.*

This is how Banff townsite might have looked a hundred years ago. Cloud covers man's intrusion, leaving only unspoiled nature unveiled.

As in the picture on the left, cloud has covered the ugly scars of development. Kananaskis Lakes photographed from Mt. Foch (3,179 m). Alberta.

The Solitary Sandpiper (Tringa solitaria) of North America on the Pacific Coast. British Columbia.

Mysterious morning scene on a pond in central British Columbia.

The winter caught autumn unawares.

Alpine world around East Lyell Glacier, Banff National Park, Alberta.

Berg Lake flanked by Mt. Robson. Mount Robson Provincial Park, British Columbia.

Caldron Lake and Peyto Peak. Banff National Park, Alberta.

Autumn image of the legendary Klondike River just east of Dawson City, Yukon Territory.

Majestic, icecapped Mt. Quadra (3,173 m) viewed from Panorama Ridge. Banff National Park, Alberta.

The monarch of the Canadian Rockies — Mt. Robson (3,954 m). Its glaciers feed the lakes and rivers of the surrounding lush meadows and rain forest. A natural paradise protected by its status as a Provincial Park. Mt. Robson Provincial Park, British Columbia.

Dall's sheep, agile and majestic inhabitants of the north, photographed on Sheep Mountain, Kluane National Park, Yukon. Glacial Slims River provides the background.

The most common member of the Jay family, the Gray Jay (Perisoreus canadensis), is found in the boreal forest throughout Canada.

The severe beauty of the wintry Rockies. On the summit of Mt. Thompson (3,063 m).
Banff National Park, Alberta.

A cascading glacier sandwiched between Mt. Shipton and Pic Tordu is part of the spectacular Clemenceau Icefield. British Columbia.

The north icefield of Mt. Athabasca (3,490 m) in autumn. Banff/Jasper National Parks, Alberta.

Moraine Lake, a green jewel of the Rockies. Valley of the Ten Peaks. Banff National Park, Alberta.

Marvel Creek and Lake. Mt. Assiniboine is hidden in clouds on the right. Banff National Park, Alberta.

Wild strawberry, a common plant with several varieties growing in western Canada.

Wild mushrooms, an attractive sight of the moist forest floor.

The rugged beauty of Bugaboo glacier enhanced by capricious mountain weather. Purcell Mountains.
British Columbia.

Morning glory over Kananaskis Country as seen from Mt. Foch (3,179 m). Kananaskis Provincial Park, Alberta.

Dawson Falls on the Murtle River. Wells Gray Provincial Park. British Columbia.

The cedar-edged Pacific coast near Port Edward. British Columbia.

Mysterious and wild, rugged and beautiful. Northern nature. Kluane Lake,
Kluane National Park, Yukon.

*Truly spectacular northern wilderness. A home for dozens of species of birds and mammals. The Mackenzie
River Delta. Northwest Territories.*

Badlands. Dinosaur Provincial Park. Southern Alberta.

Alpine meadows. Mount Revelstoke National Park, British Columbia.

The Rockwall of the Vermilion Range in its winter glory. Kootenay National Park, British Columbia.

Tumbling Glacier on Mt. Robson. Mount Robson Provincial Park, British Columbia.

Bear grass (Xerophyllum tenax) can be found in the mountains of southern Alberta and British Columbia.

Cutting through deep canyons and tundra, the mighty Hood River flows north to Coronation Gulf on the Arctic coast.

The icecapped Ramparts and Lower Amethyst Lake, source of the Astoria River.
Jasper National Park. Alberta.

Pacific shells of the British Columbia coast.

Dawson's sunstar, a voracious carnivore which preys on Pacific invertebrates.

Holly or Christmas fern (Polystichum lonchitis).

Northern wild poppies (Papaver radicatum).

Rawson Creek. Kananaskis Provincial Park, Alberta.

Bijoux Falls. Northeastern British Columbia.

A solitary climber's camp at the col between Outpost Peak (2,865 m) and Mt. Erebus (3,119 m).
Jasper National Park, Alberta.

Originating at the Lyell Icefield, Arctomy Creek flows down through the Valley of Lakes to join the North Saskatchewan River. Banff National Park, Alberta.

Many varieties of mushrooms grow in the forest.

Bull elk or wapiti (Cervus elaphus).

Winter camping on Gilmour Glacier. Mt. Baldwin in the background. Cariboo Mountains, British Columbia.

Ski trekking in the Cariboo Mountains, British Columbia. Mt. Sir Wilfrid Laurier in the background.

On the slopes of Mt. Sir Wilfrid Laurier. Mt. King in the background. Cariboo Mountains, British Columbia.

A fairy-tale mountain morning. Maligne Lake. Jasper National Park, Alberta.

A sure sign of coming spring. Horsetail. Vancouver Island.

The lush, green nature of the British Columbia rain forest.

Moricetown Canyon on the Bulkley River just north of Smithers, British Columbia.

Shadows, light and forms of nature on a tarn in British Columbia's interior.

Tiger lily (Lilium columbianum).

A carpet of wild flowers covers the mountainsides. Mount Revelstoke National Park, British Columbia.

Destructive fire gives the forest a chance to rejuvenate.

Western wood lily (Lilium philadelphicum).

The blue waters of the Vermilion River. Kootenay National Park, British Columbia.

Driftwood at the east end of Moose Lake. Mount Robson Provincial Park, British Columbia.

Wild barley.

Frosted wild rose hips.

Winter magic.

A poplar leaf trapped in ice.

Fireweed (Epilobium angustifolium), floral emblem of Yukon.

Morning frost on wild strawberry leaves.

American bison or buffalo (Bison bison) on the prairies, east of Waterton Lakes National Park, Alberta.

Marsh-marigold (Caltha palustris). Elk Island National Park, Alberta.

Altrude Lake. Kootenay National Park, British Columbia.

Willow Ptarmigan (Lagopus lagopus).

Rocky Mountain Bighorn Ram (Ovis canadensis).

Skunk cabbage (Lysichitum americanum). A fetid plant found in moist ground of southern British Columbia and along the coast.

Devil's club (Oplopemax honidum). Its long thorns, hidden by the large leaves, make walking through the underbrush hazardous.

A glacier-fed, blue jewel of Banff National Park, Alberta — Peyto Lake.

Bow Glacier and Bow Lake, where the Bow River originates. Banff National Park, Alberta.

Mountain ash (Sorbus decora).

Larch Valley near Moraine Lake. Banff National Park, Alberta.

Cormorant colony on the Pacific coast.

Steller's sea lions on the British Columbia coast.

Kathleen Lake, Kluane National Park, Yukon Territory.

Lady Evelyn Falls on the Kakisa River. Northwest Territories.

The mighty Liard River flows north to join the Mackenzie River at Fort Simpson. Northwest Territories.

Muddy spring waters of the Kicking Horse River. Wapta Falls. Yoho National Park. British Columbia.

Winter ski trekking in the Cariboo Mountains. East-central British Columbia.

Prairie crocus (Anemone patens) found on the lower slopes of mountains, as well as the foothills and prairies.

The first frost of winter adds sparkle to the autumn beauty of the leaves of a young tree.

Lawrence Grassi Alpine Hut. Clemenceau Icefield. Mt. Shipton (3,048 m) on the right. Mt. Clemenceau (3,658 m) on the left. British Columbia.

*Egypt Lake hut. Banff National Park, Alberta. A friendly home away from home for hiker,
climber and skier.*

Plunging 50 meters into the Hood River Canyon — Wilberforce Falls is the highest waterfall in the Arctic.

Dominated by Mt. Brazeau (3,470 m), Le Grand Brazeau Range and Coronet Glacier viewed from Coronet Mountain (3,152 m). Jasper National Park, Alberta.

Originating on the western slopes of the Rockies, the Kicking Horse River rushes through a natural bridge on its journey to the Pacific. Yoho National Park, British Columbia.

Slims River emptying its meltwater and silt from the huge Kaskawulsh Glacier into Kluane Lake.
Photographed from Sheep Mountain. Kluane National Park. Yukon.

This way down — Couloir 3-4, between peaks three and four of the Valley of the Ten Peaks. Moraine Lake below, Mt. Temple on the left. Banff/Kootenay National Parks.

One of the great Canadian rivers — the Fraser River near its source. Mount Robson Provincial Park.
British Columbia.

Kinney Lake and Whitehorn Mountain (3,395 m), two wonders of Mount Robson Provincial Park.
British Columbia.

Red-throated loon of the Gaviidae family (Gavia stellata), the smallest of four loon species, photographed
on the Arctic coast.

The prettiest of all jays, Steller's Jay (Cyanocitta stelleri). Found in Canada in British Columbia and southwestern Alberta.

A forty-nine kilometre walk rewards one with a view of Snake Indian Falls. Jasper National Park, Alberta.

Iron-brown water plunges down into the Hay River Canyon. Alexandra Falls. Northwest Territories.

Amethyst Lakes, the Ramparts and mountain caribou. With jagged peaks, large glaciers, lakes and rivers and rich flora and fauna, this area is truly an alpine paradise. Jasper National Park, Alberta.

Bracket fungus surrounded by bunchberry and moss.

One-flowered wintergreen (Moneses uniflora).

Photographer's Anecdotes

At the green age of 18, I already knew that the smell of resin, the whisper of mountain torrents, the sounds of the winter blizzards and the lashing, crisp, invigorating mountain winds would have to be an integral part of my destiny. I was searching for the direction to give to my life as I did not know whether I would become a music composer, a painter, a writer or a photographer as I was interested in all these creative arts. During the following years, I studied music, painted and explored various fields of the photographic world but never was I dissociated from nature and wilderness. As time went by, my love for the great outdoors only deepened until it eventually developed into a lifelong burning passion.

I had the opportunity to explore the natural wonders of our earth and immensely enjoyed the experience of being close to mother nature. When I reached the Rockies and the Pacific coastline the enchantment of the scenery brought me total fulfillment. It gave me a reason for living; a happy, rich, eventful life which I created for myself, nurtured by the fascination of these areas.

I feel very free, happy and secure in the remote wilderness. By contrast, I am frightened and lost in the 'wilderness' of some of our cities.

Once I ran into a huge Grizzly bear, nose to nose! The bear looked at me and seemed to say: "Don't worry, man, I am just an animal. I won't harm you." And it ambled off into the bush.

By contrast, I once ran into three 'men' on Fifth Avenue in New York City and this was their approach: "Hey! Man! Hand over your wallet or you're a dead man!" Now wouldn't you say that that 'grisly' Grizzly bear was rather more civilized than the humans?

We all know that in today's world, there are people who would cut down the very last tree to earn one more dollar. Others would produce telescopic rifles to shoot down the last whooping crane or eagle. We, the majority who are sober and concerned, will stop it. We will protect and preserve our nature from these unscrupulous people, for we shall survive only if nature does.

In order to produce photographs for this book, a great deal of travelling was required. South-western Canada is near at hand and easily accessible. But the North is very remote, difficult to penetrate, thus more challenging and exciting. I have travelled along the Alaska Highway several times and I tremendously enjoy the freedom of the North.

Real northern adventure starts at the beginning of the Dempster Highway. Can you imagine yourself driving a car to Inuvik? On one of my trips I set off in early autumn to conquer the North. What tremendous scenery! The Ogilvie mountains, Arctic Circle, tundra, mirror-like lakes, great rivers. This was a real northern paradise. But something was missing, I thought. What was it? Then it dawned on me: I had not seen any wild life at all. I then recalled meeting here and there along the road, big, sturdy trucks, loaded with armed-to-the-teeth characters (who call themselves hunters). I realized of course that all the wild game was off, hiding, scared to death or already dead.

I had hoped to see the Porcupine Caribou herd on its winter migration to the south but it was too early in the season and there was no sign of the beautiful animals.

After crossing the majestic Mackenzie River, I finally reached the gateway to the delta, tundra and the North: Inuvik.

The saying that God does not like photographers must be true, for after a few days of waiting in a very cold and wet environment, out of desperation, I photographed the delta from the air (plate #51), then left to return south. I crossed the Richardson Mountains, by now covered in snow and ice, and this part of the trip turned out to be very hazardous. The Eagle

Plains and Ogilvie Mountains were also in their winter garb and looked very dramatic. Despite the raging 'bush war', I was fortunate enough to see a moose, a black bear and a grizzly on the tundra. The beauty of the landscape and my northern odyssey enchanted me but the terrible condition of the road surface left me with five flat tires!

I finally crossed the Klondike River and reached the good, old and by now quite civilized Klondike Highway, then the Alaska Highway. I felt quite relieved for I can recall the days when driving those roads almost certainly meant a broken suspension, ten flat tires and a wind-shield properly peppered with holes!

Kluane National Park in the Yukon is my great old love affair. I visit this park every time I am near by.

It was here that I ran into a pack of wolves on the shores of Kluane Lake one night while photographing an incredible display of northern lights.

My two trips to the mighty Kaskawulsh Glacier never rewarded me with quality photographs due mainly to poor weather conditions, but the thrill of meeting three grizzly bears along the Slims River was reward enough for my efforts!

There is a large population of Dall's sheep in the Park and it is sheer delight to see them (Plate #37). They can easily be spotted on the mountain sides because of their snow-white coats and they can be approached at close range. Agile and fast, sheep will run and climb to the shelter of craggy walls any time they feel danger approaching.

In order to explore the tundra environment better, I travelled to Bathurst Inlet, on the central Arctic coast. This area, I was told, was a wild life paradise. Well, I must have carried bad luck in my pack for during my ten days stay all I saw was a lone musk-ox, two kilometres away, one caribou in the evening and a nesting loon (Plate #116). Flocks of birds flew high in the skies making photography useless. I went to Wilberforce Falls and Canyon on the Hood River (Plates #110 and #58) and found both quite attractive and well worth the trip.

The Arctic weather is capricious and well known for its haze and fog. I was not even treated to one spectacular sunset! Generally it was windy and quite cold and my most delightful wilderness experience was a delectable dinner of arctic char.

My contact with the original northern people was the highlight of this trip. I found these gentle people shy but warm, reserved although friendly. They are hard working and good craftsmen. A beautiful, real people, the Inuits.

One does not have to travel to the North Pole to experience great adventures in Canada. There are still many virgin spots on the maps of British Columbia and Alberta; unclimbed peaks, unexplored valleys, wild rivers.

At the east end of Maligne Lake in Jasper National Park stands Coronet Mountain, a target for me. I set out solo for the climb from the south side, starting at the Poboktan Warden Station. The going was good and eventless until I reached the base of the mountain after a 17 kilometre hike. Here I encountered very fresh evidence of bear and sure enough soon after appeared the monarch itself, right on the way I had chosen to climb the mountain. I made a lot of noise to make it clear to that bear I was coming up that way but he also made it perfectly clear to me that he was right at home and would not budge an inch. Well, that grizzly won his point: I had to add quite a few extra kilometres to my trip in order to avoid too close an encounter with him!

The climb itself was very hard and laborious but not difficult as such and I reached the summit just before sunset. After feasting my eyes on the view of Mt. Brazeau and the spectacular vista all around, I pitched my tent and went to sleep on the mountain top. The next morning was the beginning of a sunny and warm day (Plate #111). While exploring, I found the cache of the climbers' register in a small cairn. What a treat! It was the original register book brought there by the first ascent party in 1930 and its pages were studded with names of early explorers of the Rockies such as K. Gardiner, S. Hendricks, P. Prescott and others. To my surprise I was only the seventh party to climb this mountain in 54 years! A sure sign that mountaineering is still not very popular in Canada. Perhaps this is why the Canadian wilderness is so attractive? One is more likely to meet a bear or a wolf on remote trails than human beings.

While still on the bear subject may I add that fortunately bears are alive and doing well and provide us with great thrills and excitement. To illustrate this fact here is another bear story.

Where the Saskatchewan River crosses the Banff/Jasper Highway lies a beautiful alpine area circling Glacier Lake. It was early one autumn morning that I set out to climb around Mt. Lyell. At the very beginning of my hike, I met Mama bear with her two cubs. She was quite hostile but eventually let me go by. When I reached the lake, there was Papa bear waiting to greet me and he appeared very arrogant and sure of himself, but again, after a little while, I managed to slip by. It was on the upper, densely forested slopes of Arctomys Peak while hacking my way up through dense undergrowth, that I encountered Uncle bear, a large black fellow, comfortably sprawled out on the ferns, sleeping. He was barely ten meters from me. I was really shaken but with nervous concentration I slowly and quietly backed off away from that bear's sleeping chamber and believe me, you would not be holding this 'Odyssey' in your hands had that bear woken up!

I eventually reached Arctomys Peak and here a much more pleasant greeting awaited me: a large band of goats was relaxing there and they were still around next morning when I photographed this Alpine paradise (Plate #67).

There are days when one feels down and wishes to get away from it all. An ideal spot for me to go to on such days is Fay Hut, located in Prospectors Valley in Kootenay National Park. It is a remote, lovely log cabin, well hidden on the forested slope. It sits just below a large glacier and the jagged peaks of the Bow Range.

Through the years I have collected many colourful memories from the several trips I have made to this rustic hideaway.

The best time to visit Fay Hut is at low season, in late autumn or early spring. Then most likely the cabin will be all yours. One early December when the days were at their shortest, I set out for the hut. To my surprise I noticed a pair of ski tracks going up my trail. I needed solitude but it was not meant to be, I thought. Well, perhaps I would meet nice, interesting people? When I reached the junction where the Fay Hut trail turns to the right and goes straight up a slope, I noticed the ski tracks were going on along the valley floor instead. Well it seemed that I would enjoy my solitude after all. Just before coming to the hut there is a wall, a rock band with only one small gap to go through and in the winter, this passage can be very slippery and tough to negotiate. I had a fabulously quiet and warm evening at the cabin. The new air-tight woodstove pumped well; the place was cozy and I slept like a marmot. At 7:30 the next morning I heard some noise outside the hut. I was puzzled. At early dawn? In the winter? In such a remote place? Who or what could it be? Instinctively I grabbed my ice axe and opened the door carefully. Heavens! There in front of me were two men, standing motionless, speechless, looking worn and weary to say the least! It dawned on me: that ski trail I had noticed going up the valley yesterday. It must have been these two fellows who had gone the wrong way.

The stove was already lighted and a pot of steaming water happily bubbled away. Without a word I let the men in. They sat on the bench silently with their packs still on their backs. Wasting no time, I poured two cups of tea with rum. I slipped their packs off their shoulders and left them to drink their tea. After a few moments one fellow managed to utter a weak 'thank you'. That was a very close call. Being novice skiers and travelling for the first time in that area, they simply lost their way and wandered all night through the slope. They were close to the hut but the dense forest prevented them from finding it. It was the smell of the smoke from the stove which finally led them to the hut. They were certainly not equipped to spend the night in a −15°C temperature and the poor guys barely had survived the ordeal. It took at least half an hour and a few more hot drinks before they could start talking.

Moraine Lake is a landmark in Banff National Park. Across the lake and to the south, 4 kilometres behind the jagged, towering peaks, is Fay Hut.

High up on the "Ten Peaks" above Moraine Lake there was the Graham Cooper shelter for climbers. In 1982, Parks Canada replaced it with a new, large and very comfortable hut, the Neil Colgan Hut, located one kilometre to the east of the old one.

It was the attractive location and the call of the heights that lured me to visit this new hut. I set out via Prospectors Valley and Fay Hut. Higher, above 'Old Fay', mountain meadows unveiled at my feet, after came gravel moraines and a large glacier which led to Colgan Hut. I eagerly stepped upon the glacier which was dry and clear but full of crevasses. I was properly equipped and went up quite quickly. Further up on the glacier, there was a trace of new snow but as I climbed higher, the snow became deeper and deeper until after a while, as I reached the middle of the glacier, I had to cope with 25 cm snowdrifts, covering treacherous crevasses.

No 'normal' person would venture alone on a glacier. I know the risks but I am a determined 'soloist' and seldom quit a trip because of some problems, difficulties or bad weather. It took me three hours to cross the upper part of that glacier. By now I had to contend with 50 cm of snow and probed each step carefully. The bergshrund at the upper end was very dangerous and difficult to cross.

There were already three climbers at the Hut and they had watched my progress. They greeted me with the words: "Why would a man choose to kill himself in such a beautiful environment?" Frankly I found no intelligent answer to that question. I was really deeply embarrassed and that was the last time I went solo on a large glacier.

The next day these guys tied me to their rope and we set off to visit the site where the former Graham Cooper shelter had stood. The bad weather allowed me only to produce the subdued, hazy Plate #113.

On the way down we had several close calls with crevasses but being secured by the rope we all made it back safely. When we finally reached the highway at Marble Canyon, we all agreed that this had been a very scenic and pleasant Odyssey.

If you read these tales and the others I have told in my various books, you have to admit that although beautiful, exciting and tempting, the mountain environment is very dangerous, hazardous and full of traps and surprises. Maybe that is the reason why it is so challenging and intriguing to some of us.

Man invented the wheel and sliced bread. These are certainly useful and functional inventions but nature is beyond the means of man to manipulate or improve upon. Nature must be left alone, just as it is. It has its ways and it does not need the generosity of man to help it along. I thank God for the wisdom He has given man to protect areas such as the National Parks.

These reserves must be kept flourishing and alive for ever and even more wilderness areas should be set aside. Man needs that natural environment to maintain his physical and mental well being.

Nothing enriches humans more than the simple, humble beauty of nature. To me a fragile alpine flower means more than all man made beauties.

My deep respect and love for nature calls upon me to devote all my spare time to that most important and noble cause: the protection of the spectacular and in many ways unique, Western Canadian wilderness.

GEORGE BRYBYCIN

The Authors

DOROTHY DICKSON came to Canada from England twenty-two years ago and has lived in the west since 1968.

Her interest in natural history and love of the wilderness have taken her from the U.S. border to the Arctic Ocean, from the prairies to the Pacific coast. With her husband and daughters, she has explored the wild places on foot, horseback and by canoe delighting in both the rich and the intriguing scientific detail.

Realizing that unless it is protected, the wilderness is easily spoilt or destroyed by inappropriate use and that people only defend what they understand and appreciate, Dorothy has worked hard to promote and improve environmental education. For this she received an Alberta Achievement Award in 1980.

She hopes her writing will help others to value the interwoven fragility of the wilderness and respect the needs of its natural inhabitants while taking pleasure in its vast and intricate beauty.

GEORGE BRYBYCIN is one of Canada's foremost wilderness and mountain photographers. George has spent much of his adult life travelling throughout the Canadian and American west in search of adventures and challenges presented by this fabulous mountainous region.

He has climbed solo well over two hundred peaks in North America alone, in addition to ascents in Europe, Asia and Africa.

Born and educated in Europe, he grew up in the pervasive intellectual atmosphere of the old continent.

His sensitive and creative nature was enriched by extensive travels in Europe and around the world. Although a city dweller, contact with the great outdoors as a child marked him for life as a passionate naturalist.

George is the author of eleven pictorial books and possesses what could possibly be the largest one-man collection of photographs of the Rockies and western wilderness of North America. George states: "I am a wealthy man. I am rich in beautiful experiences and adventures no money can buy. My wealth needs no security men to guard it, it is in my heart, deeply enshrined in my soul."

That burning desire for 'wealth' will certainly lead George to create more heart warming photographic essays. It seems as if his wilderness odyssey has only just begun.